FRANCE

Written by
Hermione Redshaw

Gareth Stevens
PUBLISHING

Please visit our website, www.garethstevens.com. For a free color catalog of all our high-quality books, call toll free 1-800-542-2595 or fax 1-877-542-2596.

Cataloging-in-Publication Data

Names: Redshaw, Hermione, 1998-.
Title: France / Hermione Redshaw.
Description: New York : Gareth Stevens Publishing, 2024. | Series: Travel the world!
Identifiers: ISBN 9781538288337 (pbk.) | ISBN 9781538288344 (library bound) | ISBN 9781538288351 (ebook)
Subjects: LCSH: France--Juvenile literature.France--Description and travel--Juvenile literature.
Classification: LCC DC33.R437 2024 | DDC 914.404--dc23

Published in 2024 by
Gareth Stevens Publishing
2544 Clinton St.
Buffalo, NY 14224

Written by: Hermione Redshaw
Edited by: Elise Carraway
Designed by: Amy Li

Photo Credits
All images are courtesy of Shutterstock.com, unless otherwise specified. With thanks to Getty Images, Thinkstock Photo and iStockphoto. Recurring images – ONYXprj, Ihor Biliavskyi, Olleg, Looper. Cover – Alushka, Moloko88, AlinArt, Jemastock, AtlasbyAtlas Studio, Siberian Art, lemono. 2–3 – Anna_Pustynnikova. 4–5 – GoodStudio, klyaksun, narak0rn, natrot, Robert Biedermann, Stoker-13. 6–7 – alexmstudio, Arnaud Serander (Wikimedia Commons), brichuas, Everett Collection, Kirk, Fisher, klyaksun, MisterStock, Pixavril. 8–9 – ProStockStudio, andre quinou, canadastock, klyaksun, narak0rn, Pecold. 10–11 – AlinArt, Artistic Ahry, Photographer_ME, Sergii Figurnyi, WDG Photo. 12–13 – ColorMaker, HUANG Zheng, ilolab, Ji-Elle-Bourges (Wikimedia Commons), klyaksun, Modvector. 14–15 – Electric Egg, Greens87, Ihor Serdyukov, Keitma, Leonid Andronov, Pierre Jean Durieu, Richard F. Lyon (Wikimedia Commons). 16–17 – brichuas, impressions.of, Massimo Santi, ProStockStudio, Sergey Novikov, Sharon Wildie. 18–19 – Boris Stroujko, David Ridley, Dmitry Rukhlenko, klyaksun, mayalis. 20–21 – Aleksandar Todorovic, Andreas Prott, Margarita Hintukainen, proslgn, Vector_Up. 22–23 – GoodStudio, Hangouts Vector Pro, Bibadash.

Printed in the United States of America

CPSIA compliance information: Batch #CSGS24: For further information contact Gareth Stevens at 1-800-542-2595.

CONTENTS

WORDS THAT LOOK LIKE THIS CAN BE FOUND IN THE GLOSSARY ON PAGE 24.

WE ARE GOING ON A TRIP

My name is Jess. Mom, Dad, and I are getting ready to go on a road trip! There are many things to see and do on a road trip. I am looking forward to getting started!

We are going to be driving around France. France is a country in Europe. Mom and Dad promised that we would be stopping at some great places on the way. I wonder what we will see!

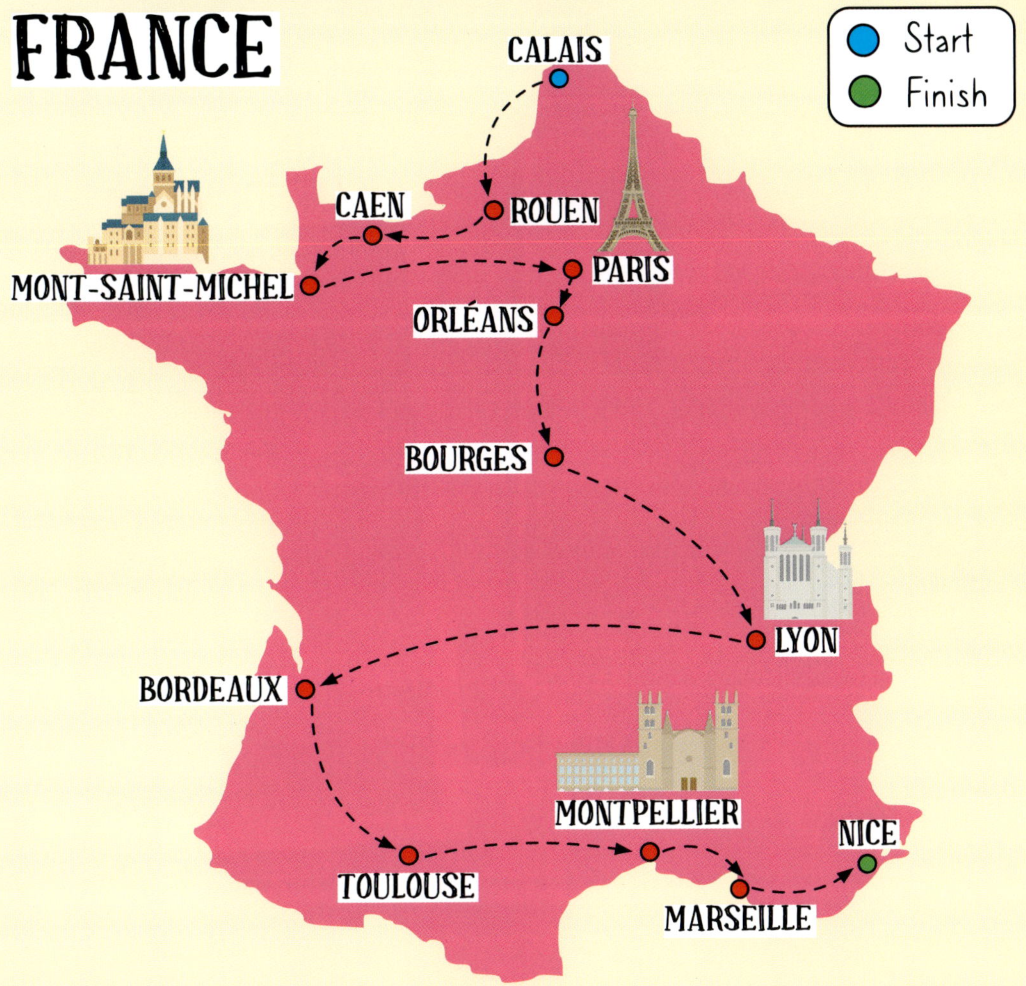

CALAIS

We start our French road trip in Calais. Calais is a port city. We see lots of big boats, called ferries. We also visit the Calais Lighthouse.

FERRY

CALAIS LIGHTHOUSE

ROUEN

The famous artist Monet painted a picture of Rouen Cathedral. We are not the only tourists wanting to see it! Then, we have a picnic in the Jardin des Plantes. Jardin is French for garden.

MONET'S PAINTING

It looks pretty good!

ROUEN CATHEDRAL

JARDIN DES PLANTES

CAEN

Caen was founded around 1,000 years ago by a man called William the Conqueror. Apparently, Caen Castle was built for him! We visit the castle's two museums. There are some important history museums in Caen.

CAEN CASTLE

MONT-SAINT-MICHEL

Mont-Saint-Michel is an island that was difficult to visit before a road was built. There is quicksand around the island! It sounds scary, but we go on a tour walking across it. It is exciting!

MONT-SAINT-MICHEL

OUR TOUR GROUP

PARIS

Paris is the capital city of France. There are so many things to see here that we cannot get to all of them! We have to see the Eiffel Tower, though!

We drive past the Arc de Triomphe!

We see Notre-Dame, which is a famous cathedral in Paris. There is some amazing art at the Louvre. We also travel just outside Paris to visit the Palace of Versailles.

NOTRE-DAME

THE LOUVRE

PALACE OF VERSAILLES

ORLÉANS

Orléans has a museum about Joan of Arc. Joan was an important person in the history of France. She helped to protect Orléans when she was about 17 years old. It is interesting learning about her!

JOAN OF ARC MUSEUM

MONUMENT OF JOAN OF ARC IN ORLÉANS

BOURGES

There are buildings that are hundreds of years old in some parts of Bourges, such as the Old Town and the Promenade des Remparts. It feels like we stepped back in time!

PROMENADE DES REMPARTS

OLD TOWN

LYON

Lyon used to be part of the Roman Empire. There are many things left in the city from that time. We find two old Roman theaters! The Roman museum helps to explain Lyon's Roman history.

ANCIENT THEATER OF FOURVIÈRE

THE ODEON

THE ROMAN MUSEUM

After all that history, we go to the Parc de la Tête d'Or. There are lots of fun things here for kids. We take the park train, go on the merry-go-round, and even drive some go-karts!

MERRY-GO-ROUND

BORDEAUX

There is a mirror of water in Bordeaux, called the Miroir d'Eau. It sits in front of the Place de la Bourse. The pool makes the buildings reflect upside down in the water!

TOULOUSE

Toulouse is sometimes called the Pink City. There are so many pink buildings here, including shops and churches. We visit the Cité de l'Espace, which is a museum about space. There are rides there too!

A ROCKET IN THE CITÉ DE L'ESPACE

MONTPELLIER

There are plenty of places to see animals in Montpellier. We go to the Montpellier Zoo. It is like a safari park! We eat ice cream while watching giraffes eat leaves from tall trees.

MARSEILLE

Marseille has a fortress called the Château d'If. The fortress sits on a small island in the water. We have to take a boat out to see it. You can see the whole city of Marseille from the island.

CHATEÂU D'IF

MARSEILLE FROM FAR AWAY

NICE

FLOWERS AT THE MARKET

The last stop on our road trip around France is Nice. We visit the Cours Saleya, which is a market in the old part of Nice. There are lots of fresh food and pretty flowers.

COURS SALEYA MARKET

We ride bicycles down the Promenade des Anglais. The Promenade is right next to the sea. We relax on the beach and swim in the water. It is great!

BICYCLE PATHS ON THE PROMENADE DES ANGLAIS

HOME

France was great fun! From Calais to Nice, there were so many incredible things to do and see. We explored some beautiful cities, found out about some interesting history, and relaxed on the beach.

We could not see everything in France. I wish we could have visited the Luxembourg Gardens or seen the Arch of Germanicus.

Love, Jess

BONJOUR!
FROM
Paris

GLOSSARY

CATHEDRAL an important church building

FORTRESS a place that is protected

FOUNDED began or created

PORT somewhere ships stop to load and unload things

QUICKSAND deep, wet sand into which heavy objects sink easily

REFLECT to show a mirrored image of something

ROMAN EMPIRE a large area that was once under the control of the Romans

SAFARI driving around to see animals

THEATER a place where plays and shows are performed on a stage

INDEX